The Greatest Money-Making Secret in History!

By

Joe Vitale

Author of the #1 best-seller, *Spiritual Marketing*, and way too many other books to list here

ISBN: 1-4107-4117-6 (e-book)
ISBN: 1-4107-4116-8 (Paperback)
ISBN: 1-4107-4115-X (Dust Jacket)

Library of Congress Control Number: 2003092372

This book is printed on acid free paper.

Printed in the United States of America
Bloomington, IN

Cover cartoon by Sean D'Souza of www.psychotactics.com
Proofreading by Jenny Meadows.
Back Cover photograph by Nerissa Oden.

1stBooks – rev. 04/04/03

This publication is designed to provide accurate information in regard to the subject matter covered. It is offered with the understanding that the author and publisher are not engaged in rendering medical or psychological service. This book is not intended to be a substitute for therapy or professional advice.

To contact the author of this book,
please email *giving@mrfire.com*
or visit his website at www.mrfire.com

To order more copies of this book,
please visit www.amazon.com
or www.1stbooks.com
or call 1-888-280-7715

Dedication

This book is dedicated to John Harricharan,
best-selling author, spiritual advisor and dear friend
– a man who has given freely his entire life.

Table of Contents

"If ever there is a lack of any kind, whether it is need for employment, or for money, or for guidance, or even for healing, <u>something is blocking the flow</u>. And the most effective remedy: Give!"

—Eric Butterworth, *Spiritual Economics: The Prosperity Process*

The Power of Giving

An Introduction

By John Harricharan

It was a really hot summer's day many years ago. I was on my way to pick up two items at the grocery store. In those days, I was a frequent visitor to the supermarket because there never seemed to be enough money for a whole week's food-shopping at once.

You see, my young wife, after a tragic battle with cancer, had died just a few months earlier. There was no insurance—just many expenses and a mountain of bills. I held a part-time job, which barely generated enough money to feed my two young children. Things were bad—really bad.

And so it was that day, with a heavy heart and four dollars in my pocket, I was on my way to the supermarket to purchase a gallon of milk and a loaf of bread. The children were hungry and I had to get them something to eat. As I came to a red traffic light, I noticed on my right a young man, a young woman and a child on the grass next to the road. The blistering noonday sun beat down on them without mercy.

The man held up a cardboard sign which read, "Will Work for Food." The woman stood next to him. She just stared at the cars stopped at the red light. The child, probably about two years old, sat on the grass holding a one-armed doll. I noticed all this in the thirty seconds it took for the traffic light to change to green.

I wanted so desperately to give them a few dollars, but if I did that, there wouldn't be enough left to buy the milk and bread. Four dollars will only go so far. As the light changed, I took one last glance at the three of them and sped off feeling both guilty (for not helping them) and sad (because I didn't have enough money to share with them).

As I kept driving, I couldn't get the picture of the three of them out of my mind. The sad, haunting eyes of the young man and his family stayed with me for about a mile. I could take it no longer. I felt their pain and had to do something about it. I turned around and drove back to where I had last seen them.

I pulled up close to them and handed the man two of my four dollars. There were tears in his eyes as he thanked me. I smiled and drove on to the supermarket. Perhaps both milk and bread would be on sale, I thought. And what if I only got milk alone, or just the bread? Well, it would have to do.

I pulled into the parking lot, still thinking about the whole incident, yet feeling good about what I had done. As I stepped out of the car, my foot slid on something on the pavement. There by my feet was a twenty-dollar bill. I just couldn't believe it. I looked all around, picked it up with awe, went into the store and purchased not only bread and milk, but several other items I desperately needed.

I never forgot that incident. It reminded me that the universe was strange and mysterious. It confirmed my belief that you could never out give the universe. I gave away two dollars and got twenty in return. On my way back from the supermarket, I drove by the hungry family and shared five additional dollars with them.

This incident is only one of many that have occurred in my life. It seems that the more we give, the more we get. It is, perhaps, one of those universal laws that say, "If you want to receive, you must first give."

There is a little rhyme that goes like this:

"A man there was, and they called him mad,
The more he gave, the more he had."

Most times, we think that we don't have anything to give. Yet, if we look more closely, we'll see that even the little we have could be shared with others. Let us not wait for a time when we think we'll have lots and then we'll give. By giving and sharing the little we have, we open up the storehouse of the universe and permit rivers of good to come our way.

Don't take my word for it. Just honestly try to give and you'll be surprised at the results. Generally, the returns do not come back from those we give to. It comes back from sources we could hardly imagine. So give your way to riches.

Take a chance on this universal principle. Take a chance on yourself. Universal principles always work.

Sometimes the return from giving happens very quickly as in the true story above. Other times, it takes much longer. But be assured of this: Give and you will receive—and you'll receive lots more than you ever gave.

And when you give, don't do it with a heart of fear, but with a heart full of gratitude. You will be amazed at how it all works out. Open the gates of affluence in your life by giving a bit of what you have to those in need. As the great Teacher said, "Give and it will be given unto you."

Try it. You'll like it.

John Harricharan is the award-winning author of "When You Can Walk on Water, Take the Boat." See a free sample download at http://www.waterbook.com. Also visit http://www.insight2000.com and http://www.powerpause.com

The Greatest Money-Making
Secret in History!

If you want money, you only have to do one thing.

It's the one thing some of the wealthiest people on the planet have done and are doing.

It's the one thing written about in various ancient cultures and still promoted today.

It's the one thing that will bring money to anyone who does it but at the same time most people will fear doing it.

What is that one thing?

John D. Rockefeller did it since he was a child. He became a billionaire.

Andrew Carnegie did it, too. He became a tycoon.

What is the greatest money-making secret in history?

What is the one thing that works for everyone?

Give money away.

That's right. Give it away.

Give it to people who help you stay in touch with your inner world.

Give it to people who inspire you, serve you, heal you, love you.

Give it to people without expecting them to return it, but give it knowing it will come back to you multiplied from some source.

In 1924 John D. Rockefeller wrote to his son and explained his practice of giving away money. He wrote, "...in the beginning of getting money, away back in my childhood, I began giving it away, and continued increasing the gifts as the income increased..."

Did you notice what he said?

He gave away more money as he received more income. He gave away $550 million dollars in his lifetime.

Some people think Rockefeller started giving away dimes as a publicity stunt to improve his image. That's not true. The public relations man who worked for Rockefeller was Ivy Lee. In *Courtier To The Crowd*, a great biography of Lee, Ray Eldon Hiebert states Rockefeller had been giving money away for decades on his own. All Lee did was let the public know.

P.T. Barnum gave money away, too. As I wrote in my book on him, *There's A Customer Born Every Minute*, Barnum believed in what he called a "profitable philanthropy." He knew giving would lead to receiving. He, too, became one of the world's richest men.

Andrew Carnegie gave enormously, too. Of course, he became one of the richest men in America's history.

Bruce Barton, cofounder of the famous BBDO advertising agency and the key subject of my book *The Seven Lost Secrets of Success*, also believed in giving. In 1927 he wrote:

"If a man practices doing things for other people until it becomes so much a habit that he is unconscious of it, all the good forces of the universe line up behind him and whatever he undertakes to do."

Barton became a best-selling author, business celebrity, contributor to numerous causes, and very, very, wealthy.

While some might argue that these early tycoons had the money to give, so it was easy for them, I would argue that they got the money in part because they were willing to freely give. The giving led to the receiving. The giving led to more wealth.

I'll repeat that:

The giving led to the receiving.

The giving led to more wealth.

Today it's fashionable for businesses to give money to worthy causes. It makes them look good and of course it helps those who receive it. Anita Roddick's Body Shop stores, Ben Cohen and Jerry Greenfield's ice cream, and Yvon Chouinard's Patagonia, are living examples of how giving can be good for business.

But what I'm talking about here is individual giving. I'm talking about you giving money so you will receive more money.

If there's one thing I think people do wrong when they practice giving, is they give too little. They hold on to their money and let it trickle out when it comes to giving. And that's why they aren't receiving. You have to give, and give a lot, to be in the flow of life to receive.

I remember when I first heard about the idea of giving. I thought it was a scheme to get me to give money to the people who were telling me to do the giving.

If I did give, it was like a miser. Naturally, what I got in return was equivalent to what I gave. I gave little. I got little.

But then one day I decided to test the theory of giving.

I love inspiring stories. I read them, listen to them, share them, and tell them. I decided to thank Mike Dooley of www.tut.com for the inspiring messages he shares with me and others every day by email.

I decided to give him some money. In the past I would have given him maybe five dollars. But that's when I came from scarcity and feared the giving principle wouldn't work. This time would be different. I took out my checkbook and wrote a check for one thousand dollars.

It was the largest single contribution I had ever made in my life at that time.

Yes, it made me a tiny bit nervous. But it mostly made me excited. I wanted to make a difference. I wanted to reward Mike. And I wanted to see what would happen.

Mike was stunned. He got my check in the mail and nearly drove off the road as he headed home. He couldn't believe it. He even called me and thanked me. I enjoyed his boyish surprise. It made me feel like a million bucks. *(Note that!)*

I loved making him so happy. I delighted in giving the money to him. Whatever he did with it was fine with me. What I got was an incredible feeling of helping someone continue doing what I believed in. It was an inner rush to help him. I still rejoice at sending him the money.

And then something wonderful began to happen.

I suddenly got a call from a person who wanted me to co-author his book, a job that ended up paying me many times over what I had given away.

And then a publisher in Japan contacted me, wanting to buy the translation rights to my best-selling book, *Spiritual Marketing*. They, too, offered me many times what I had given Mike as a gift.

A true skeptic can say these events are not related. Maybe in the skeptic's mind, they aren't. In mine, they are.

When I gave money to Mike, I sent a message to myself and to the world that I was prosperous and in the flow. I also set up a magnetic principle that attracted money to me: As you give, so you will get.

Give time and you'll get time.

Give products and you'll get products.

Give love and you'll get love.

Give money and you'll get money.

This one tip alone can transform your finances. Think of the person or persons who have inspired you over the last week. Who made you feel good about yourself, your life, your dreams, or your goals?

5

Give that person some money. Give them something from your heart. Don't be stingy. Come from abundance, not scarcity. Give without expecting return from that person, but do expect return.

As you do, you will see your own prosperity grow.

That's the Greatest Money-Making Secret in History!

"If you see it, touch it.
If you touch it, feel it.
If you feel it, love it.
If you love it…Give it."

Because NOTHING speaks to the UNIVERSE louder,
of your BELIEF in self, abundance, and love, than giving.

And when the Universe hears, more will be added unto you.
NOT AS A REWARD, but because you truly believed…in self,
abundance, and love.

—from www.tut.com

The Great Secret To
Activating The Law

The lady on the phone had a question.

"I've been giving money away for years and I haven't seen my own prosperity grow at all. What am I doing wrong?"

"Where are you giving money?"

"To my local church."

"Why are you giving them money?" I asked.

"They need it."

"How do you feel when you give it to them?"

"Like I am helping them out of a hole."

"But how do you *really* feel when you give them money?"

There was a moment of silence.

"Well, it's a pain," she admitted. "I cringe when I write them a check."

Not good.

"If you feel lousy when you give money, then you are associating money with bad feelings," I explained. "You probably don't want to

7

attract more bad feelings, so you probably won't attract much more money, either."

"Wow. I never thought of it that way."

"And if you give because someone asked for it or even pleaded for it, then you are reinforcing need," I explained. "In order for you to experience increased wealth, you want to give money wherever it makes you feel good to do so. In other words, giving to someone who needs it is a noble thing to do. Do it. But that's not the principle I'm talking about here."

"I get it!" she said. I couldn't help but think some other part of the universe was helping her understand what I couldn't explain.

"What did you get?" I asked.

"I've been keeping the church in a begging mode," she said. "My heart wants to give money to wherever I feel spiritual nourishment. Sometimes that's my church. Sometimes it's not."

"You got it!" I said.

And there you have it.

You can give money to any causes you like. I've helped The Red Cross, the Make-A-Wish Foundation, cancer funds, and more. But I didn't expect my finances to increase from that giving. That generosity was helping, yes, but not necessarily activating spiritual law.

The spiritual law of financial income seems to happen when you give money freely to wherever you get your spiritual nourishment, with a small expectation that somehow, some way, some day, your finances will increase as a result.

Giving to worthy causes might activate the law if you feel you received spiritual nourishment from those causes. But if you didn't, and you give anyway, you are probably just helping people in need. That, of course, is noble. I say do it.

Again, the subject of this book is the greatest money-making secret in history. And you activate that secret when you give freely, joyously, to wherever you currently get spiritual nourishment and nurturing.

"Money is an outer form of spiritual substance."
—Georgiana Tree West, *Prosperity's Ten Commandments*

The Great Back-Door
Secret to Wealth

I received a check in the mail today from a long-lost friend.

The check is for only a portion of the money he owes me. But since he took almost ten years to send this amount, I am glad to see it.

Ten years ago he hired me to write a detailed marketing strategy for him. At that time, I charged a few thousand dollars for such a service. He agreed to it and said he would pay. I did the work and he didn't pay.

Because he was my friend, I let the invoice slide. Months went by. Then years. Then he moved to another state. And I moved to another city. He went on his way in life and basically dropped out of my awareness. I went on my own way and fairly quickly became somewhat famous on the Internet for my books and tapes.

One day a few months ago I received an email from someone who wanted to co-author a book with me. He said he knew some of my friends, and mentioned the one who owed me money.

As soon as I saw my old friend's name, my blood pressure rose. I felt myself get angry. I felt ripped off. Betrayed. Hurt.

I took some deep breaths and calmed myself down. I talked to myself. I reminded myself that the universe is a big place (some understatement) and that wealth can come from many avenues, not just from past invoices. I decided to forgive my friend. And I did, mentally. I sincerely let him and his debt go. I didn't need the money. And I didn't need to be right.

After maybe nine years, my friend sent me an email. He said he knew he owed me money. He explained that he had tough times, that he had moved, that he was trying to make it as a professional speaker. He added that he wanted to bring peace to our old friendship.

I wrote him a brief note saying we already had peace. I also invited him to pay off his invoice by sending me a check for a tiny percentage of what he owed me (about twenty percent, as I recall). He agreed.

Well, he didn't send me a check. Not right away, anyway. Several more months passed before I heard from him again. This time it was another email, and this time he was again explaining his situation to me.

I remained at peace. I knew I would have money. It didn't have to come from him. The universe—whatever you want to call that power bigger than you or I—would see that money came to me as long as I stayed in the flow. And being at peace is a good way to stay in the flow.

And, as I explained in the beginning of this chapter, the check arrived today.

I have no idea how my old friend felt as he wrote that check. I hope he did it with a heart full of joy. If so, he activated the money-attracting principle.

I know when I wrote a check for $500 to my brother, who had helped me out of a bind twenty years before and I finally paid him off, I felt *exhilarated.* Writing that check to Ted made me feel like a king. And it gave me such an inner sense of peace that that alone was worth a million dollars.

I'm calling this sense of peace—or forgiveness, if you will—a back-door secret to wealth.

Where in your life are you holding grudges because someone owes you money? Or maybe because you owe someone money?

Let it go. Talk to yourself. Allow yourself the heavenly awareness that the universe provides, not your friends. Money doesn't come to you from them, it comes to you *through* them.

Once you can let the grudges go, you free yourself to receive.

Beware This Great Trap

The article that gave birth to this book was called "The Greatest Money-Making Secret in History," which was a shorter version of chapter one.

That article became so popular that it was distributed to thousands of people across the Internet. Ezine publishers reproduced and distributed it. Content websites stored the article on their sites. And dozens of people wrote me, most thanking me and praising the article.

But a few of the emails I received were curious. They were from people asking me for money.

Apparently they read my article and concluded that I was someone who would give money to anyone who asked for it. So they wrote and asked for it.

The problem is, that's not what the article describes as the great secret for attracting wealth. I never wrote, "Ask for money and you'll get wealthy." Instead I conveyed the message, "Give money to wherever you received spiritual nourishment and you'll activate the money-attracting law."

I wrote to every person who had written to me asking for money. I explained the concept.

None of them wrote back.

I'm bringing this experience up for you to consider for two reasons:

1. Don't beg for money and expect to get wealthy. Just look at the beggars on the streets. They are not living prosperous life styles. They are just getting by, if that. Or look at the people who do fund-raising. Most of them are begging, though they would never call it that, and they never seem to have enough. Is that a clue or what?

2. Don't give money to beggars and expect to get wealthy. I didn't say don't help the poor, though it's questionable how much it helps them to hand them things. Instead, I'm saying don't give money to people just because they ask for it and expect to turn on the universe's cornucopia.

I see giving money out of a sense of obligation or duty as a trap.

That was always the problem I had with ministers who asked people to give money because either (a) they needed it or (b) the Bible decreed it.

Either may be true. But if you or anyone gives money without a feeling of joy in your heart, it is highly unlikely that the money you gave will come back to you multiplied.

The best way to determine where to give money is to ask yourself one simple question:

Where did you receive the most joy?

And if you want further clarity, or more questions to assist you in knowing where to give money, try these on for size:

Where were you reminded of your divinity?

Where were you encouraged to go for your dreams?

Who made you feel glad to be alive?

Whatever your answer, *that's* where to give your money.

"Many people have had a psychological block against tithing (giving), because so many theologians have stressed what tithing would do for the church rather than what it could do for the individual."

—Catherine Ponder, *Open Your Mind to Prosperity*

My Great Confession

Okay, I'll confess.

I found it hard to believe I would receive money if I gave money.

It just sounded like such a con, like a strategy promoted by people who wanted me to give money *to them*.

Well, I was too smart for that.

I decided that I would not give money, but that I would instead give books.

That's right. Books. I had plenty of books. Since I had worked as a New Age journalist and book reviewer for many years, I had collected a lot of books. I had more than I needed. Why not give some of them away?

I still remember making the decision. I was lying in bed in Houston, where I lived at the time, reflecting on how to get prosperous.

I remember thinking, "I can become the richest man in America in terms of books."

And right then and there I decided to try out the giving principle on books.

Within days I had called a few friends over and let them pick out books. I didn't let them pick out any books or all my books, of course. But I pulled a few piles of books out and let my friends take what they wanted.

Then, over the course of the next few months, whenever I gave a talk someplace, I also gave out books. I found it a terrific way to hold attention. Whenever someone's attention seemed to wander, I announced a free book for the next person who asked me a question. Everyone in the room perked up.

And when I moved into this country estate where I now live, I set about 25 boxes of books in the garage. I then threw a house-warming party and had people come over. I told them that before they left, they were encouraged to go through the boxes and take what they wanted. Everyone did. One person took so many books that he needed a dolly to wheel them to his car.

What was the result of my grand book-giving?

Ever since the day in Houston when I decided to give books to receive books, I have always had an abundance of books.

And today I own one of the largest book collections in the world on marketing, and another on metaphysics.

People see my collection whenever they visit here and are in awe.

What they don't understand is this:

Books will always come to me because I always give books.

I was activating the great giving principle, but on books.

Today I know to give money to receive money. And as a result, I have money, far more than I ever did when I lived in Houston.

But in those early days, when I feared losing money and wanted to hold on to all I had, all I could allow myself to give were books.

As a result, books came.

Listen and learn: *Give* what you want *to receive.*

"We must not try to fix the avenues through which our good is to come. There is no reason for thinking that what you give will come back through the one to whom you gave it."

—Charles Fillmore, *Prosperity*

The Great Man Who Gave Away
30 Million Dollars

I just learned that a famous, colorful and charming American philanthropist is dead.

I had always loved his book, *Ask for the Moon and Get It: The Secret to Getting What You Want by Knowing How to Ask.*

His name was Percy Ross. Maybe you heard of him. Ross gave away an estimated thirty million dollars to various charities and organizations. He also wrote a syndicated newspaper column, called *Thanks a Million*, for approximately 800 nationwide newspapers for 17 years. The column contained letters from people writing Ross, telling him their story and asking for his help. It was fascinating.

It was fascinating because Ross could always see through people. He would read their letters and sense if they were sincere, or lazy, or begging. And he always replied with words of wisdom—and sometimes with a check. He gave checks 120 times per week. And in 17 years he gave away about $30,000,000.

The thing is, Ross started with *two* million dollars!

19

Do you see the giving principle at work here?

Ross began with two million dollars as his source funds. You may not have that amount, but the story still holds true. In 17 years Ross gave away *thirty* million dollars!

Again, giving leads to receiving.

Consider: Have you ever experienced a situation where you were asked to donate money to a particular cause, and looking at your shrinking bank balance you were torn between giving money or not? Many people have told me stories about being in this exact situation, but after deciding to go ahead and make a donation, these same people were very surprised when suddenly a sum of money came to them from some unexpected source to replace the money they just gave away.

The truth is, if you hold on to your money, you risk losing the very thing you are hoarding. On the other hand, if you trust good things flow to those who give freely, you will always have funds available to suit your needs.

To prove this, look at Percy Ross. He started his charitable ways with $2 million and yet over the course of 17 years donated some $30 million!

I miss Percy Ross.

But now *you* can take his place.

What is True Giving?
Or, Do You Have An
"Equation Mentality"?

I just got off the phone with my dear friend, Dr. Paul Hartunian, publicity genius, philanthropist and true lover of dogs.

I asked Paul about giving and how he saw it working in his own life and with his own personal cause. That's when he told me something truly eye-opening.

"Too many people make an equation out of giving," he said. "They give some money and then wait for it to come back to them ten-fold. That, to me, is not true giving."

This was a shocking statement to me.

"What is true giving then?" I asked.

"I believe true giving is done anonymously," Paul explained. "If someone gives a million dollars to a foundation because they are going to have a building named after them, then that is trading, not giving."

Paul was bringing up a valid point.

I remember a time when someone e-mailed me, asking what they should do if they try to give money to their friends and it's refused. I remember thinking, *Why do your friends have to know it's coming from you? Can't you give in secret?*

Paul went on to tell me something even more fascinating.

"I think the secret to giving is in not caring if it comes back to you or not," he explained. "Once you don't care, you're in the flow."

Ah, yes!

That's the secret!

Give without expecting return—give because your heart moves you to give—give because it's your joy to give—and you're in the flow of life itself.

"All I can say is that maybe the Cosmos handles the rest," Paul told me. "I've been blessed in my life but I didn't give to be blessed. The cosmos just took care of me."

I love how Paul Hartunian explained all of this to me. He gave such a practical, level-headed view of giving.

"I have no problem with someone being recognized for giving," he added. "But if you give *because* you want recognition or you expect a ten-fold return, then you're not giving, you're calculating."

Paul walks his talk. Around Christmas of 2002 he sent me an email and asked if I had anything of a spiritual nature he could give to the readers of his e-newsletter. He said he always gave them publicity and money-making advice. Now he wanted to give them something spiritual.

I suggested he let his fans read the e-book version of my #1 best-seller, *Spiritual Marketing*. I told him anyone could read the e-version online at http://www.mrfire.com/spirit

Paul let his readers know. He was very generous to do so. After all, he didn't make a dime off my book and never would from this endorsement. He was simply giving.

Now the punch line here is that Paul had, at that time, about 76,000 readers. That meant his gift (and my gift, too) touched a lot of lives. Paul gave from his heart. I gave from my heart. How this will come back to us, no one knows—except maybe the Cosmos.

Are you giving?

"The law of prosperity, whose first action is giving, comes so close into the heart of being that we can scarcely expect to weigh and balance it by numbers and calculations...We must give without expectation of return."

—Ernest C. Wilson, *The Great Physician*

Show Me The Money!

Am I the only one who *really* saw the movie *Jerry McGuire*?

That hit movie starring Tom Cruise had everyone repeating the famous line, *"Show me the money!"*

I didn't watch the movie for nearly one year after it was released because I thought it was all about greed. Since everyone who saw the movie smiled and repeated that one line—*"Show me the money!"*—as if it were some sort of national mantra, I wasn't interested.

But then one day Nerissa and I wanted to watch something on television. As luck would have it, *Jerry McGuire* was coming on the tube right about then. So we settled in to watch it.

I was amazed. The movie wasn't about greed at all. Yes, Jerry came from a money-hungry place, but he soon learned that that mindset wasn't going to work.

Greed was out.

Greed was a dead-end street.

Greed led to a poverty of spirit.

Instead, Jerry the sports agent learns about the power of passion. When he truly starts to care for his client, to look for and activate the heart in the one player he represents (who does the same for him), then and only then does he start to taste real success and start to experience real happiness.

Oh, there's no doubt the refrain *"Show me the money!"* is a catchy one. It's done so well in the movie, and said so often, and delivered with such upbeat emotion in the one unforgettable scene, that you can't *help* but remember it.

But that's not what the movie is about. Not to me. The movie is about show me your *heart*, not show me your money.

Giving is like that.

If you give because you want money, you are not giving but simply trading.

If you give because your heart sings to do so, then you are truly giving.

It's the difference between *"Show me the money!"* and *"Show me your heart."*

The universe responds to your heart, not your money. The money is just a symbol.

Give money from your heart.

When you do, very quickly and in the most surprising ways, the universe itself will then *"Show you the money!"*

But don't give to get. Don't give as a negotiation with the universe.

Give to *give*.

The Greatest Spiritual
Mind Treatment

May I offer you a gentle reminder of how the principle of giving works?

I went online and created the following short "Spiritual Mind Treatment" specifically for you. You can go to the same forms I did and create one even more personal and relevant for you. Just go online to http://www.wmop.org/Smt.htm

A "Spiritual Mind Treatment" or affirmative prayer is "...a recognition of Spirit's Omniscience, Omnipotence, and Omnipresence, and a realization of humanity's unity with Spirit..." (Ernest Holmes, *Science of Mind* textbook, pg. 149.)

That may be more than you or I can understand, so let's just call a Spiritual Mind Treatment a formula for getting in tune with the infinite. Call it magic. Call it a reminder. Call it a lucky charm. It doesn't really matter.

"Treatment is not trying to make yourself believe something that is not so, but is based upon truth," wrote Robert Bitzer in *Collected*

Essays of Robert Bitzer. "It is to change your belief so that you can recognize and accept the truth."

In other words, a treatment is a way to remind yourself of what already exists. For example, the law of giving already exists. It is truth. A treatment would be to remind you of that fact.

You can say the words below at night, in the morning, to yourself, or out loud. Most importantly, whenever you are about to give money away, say these words (or ones of your own that have meaning for you):

"I know there is an infinite energy system in the universe that is of me, in me and around me. We are all connected to it, are in it, and are of it. I am connected to you as well as to everyone else through the energy that sustains us. I know that when I give anything into this energy system, it will return to me in kind, multiplied and amplified because the nature of the system is to grow and expand. I am grateful for this realization, and for the gifts I have now, am receiving, and will receive. I trust the process to work for me, as it does for everyone who activates it with giving. So be it. It is so!"

As always, how you feel as you say those words is what matters most. Emotion activates the law.

Feel *joyous*.

How To Think Like God

About ten years ago I gave a talk entitled "How to Think Like God." People loved it. The few who were there that day in Houston still remember it. And last year I put the talk online, where anyone could listen to it over the Internet. Everyone loves it.

The reason it has such broad appeal is it's so freeing. "Thinking like God" is all about no-boundary thinking. Do you really think God would have limits? Do you really think God would talk about lack and limitation? Do you really think God would have excuses for not doing things?

I don't think so.

In my talk I told stories about Barry Neil Kaufman and his wife, Susie, healing their son of autism.

I also talked about Meir Schnieder, born blind and diagnosed as incurable, who now sees and helps others to gain or regain their vision.

And I talked about my work with Jonathan, the miracles coach I had worked with years ago. (Most of the stories are in my book *Spiritual Marketing.*)

The point here is this: If you were to pretend you could think like God, how would you think? What would you do? What would you say?

I'm pretty sure God wouldn't balk at giving money (or anything else).

I'm pretty sure God wouldn't worry about how money would come to Him (or Her).

I'm pretty sure God wouldn't put a limit on what He/She gave, either.

So: *What would you do if you thought like God?*

This wonderful question spills over into every area of your life.

How would you act in your relationships if you thought like God?

How would you act at work if you thought like God?

How would you behave in society if you thought like God?

This is more than a liberating exercise in creative imaging. This is a chance to expand your heart, too.

How do you think like God?

You pretend.

You pretend you *are* God.

If you were God, how would you think?

Personally, I don't think with *any* limitations at all when I start to role-play thinking like God.

My mind starts to consider anything and everything: Cure cancer? Of course! Win millions in the lottery? Easy! Solve world hunger? No sweat!

Of course, implementing those wide-reaching goals is another story.

So let's bring it back home, to the individual, to you, and to me.

If *I* thought like God in my own life, what would I do different?

Well, this book is a good example.

I spoke to John Harricharan on Friday afternoon. He's a dear friend and spiritual advisor. He was in one of his psychic places that day and told me I would soon write another book.

You don't have to be psychic to know that, of course. I'm an author. I'll always write another book.

But something in me triggered when John said another book was coming. We talked about book ideas for a few minutes. He pointed out how popular my article had been, the one titled, "The Greatest Money-Making Secret in History." He said a book on that would help the world, and be very welcome.

While I hadn't told John this before, I had wanted to write a book based on my article. John's gentle push was all I needed.

I started writing the book the very next day. As I type these words it is now Monday—three days later.

In short, by thinking like God, I removed all limits to how long it takes to write a book.

This one was done over a weekend, more or less.

Not bad.

Back to you: If you thought like God, what would you do right now?

If it's give money, go give it.

If it's write a book, start typing.

If it's start a business, get going.

There are no limits.

Just *think like God*.

*"In my personal experience, the reasons for tithing were never explained clearly enough, and there was always so much pressure from the head of the church that it never seemed like a free-will gift, given in loving gratitude, but rather just another bill we had to pay. Because of that attitude, tithing usually doesn't have the effect of opening the prosperity flow. The attitude, motive and Spirit with which we give this money back to the Universe is the most important thing about our gift. Our motivation **must** be that **the money we are giving away is a gift of love we are giving back to the Universe in gratitude and appreciation for our gift of life.**"*

—Patricia Diane Cota-Robles, *It Is Time For You To Be Financially Free!*

Leo Buscaglia's Big Mistake

I met Leo Buscaglia many years ago. He was the charming, passionate, and colorful author of the best-selling book, *Love*. He once said in a lecture, "I own the copyright on love!"

He was a loveable man. His words warmed my heart and inspired my soul. Marian, my wife at the time, and I used to watch Leo on television. He inspired us.

We were learning about tithing at the time. I was very skeptical. I still thought giving was a scheme. But Marian was always more open-minded and trusting than me. She practiced giving more than I did in those early years.

One day, when Marian looked around to see who she was going to send money to, she easily remembered Leo Buscaglia. She wanted to thank him for all his sharing, and for reminding her through his books and talks to always live a life of love.

So Marian found his address and sent him a check. I remember how happy she looked as she wrote him a note and mailed him the gift. Her heart was alive.

But then something sad happened.

A few weeks later, Marian received a letter from Leo Buscaglia. He had returned her check. He added a note that said he had plenty and didn't want or need more, so please give the check to someone in need.

Marian was hurt. She was offended. She felt rejected. She saw the refusal of the gift as a dismissal of her. It was a sad moment.

While we could talk about Marian's response to the letter she received, my point here is more about Leo's action. I think Leo made a mistake. In order to be in the flow of life, you must give as well as receive. Leo cut off the flow.

Much later I learned—from Leo himself—that he had experienced several robberies. His house had been broken into and his belongings taken. It happened to him at least twice that I recall.

I can't help but think Leo had inner blocks about receiving. Those blocks showed up in his outer world by losing all he had. I could be wrong, but I really wonder if there was a connection between his refusing gifts and losing what he had.

Let's learn from Leo's mistake.

When someone offers you money, accept it.

When someone offers you a compliment, accept it.

When someone offers you any gift, joyfully welcome it.

If you refuse gifts, compliments, and money, you are closing a door on the prosperity that is trying to come to you. The key is to be in the flow. When you give *and* receive, you are participating in the flow of life.

After all, money has to circulate to do everyone any good.

Give it.

And when it returns to you, *receive it*.

Does Free Have Value?

There's a theory in marketing that people don't appreciate what they get for free.

Is that true?

While it is true that the word "Free" is probably the most powerful and persuasive word someone can use in their marketing, it may also be true that anything someone receives for free is usually treated with disregard or disrespect.

This has been proven over and over again. Consultants who give their time and services away often find the people who received their gifts don't appreciate them. In general, only when someone pays for something do they pay attention to it.

But is that true in the art of giving money?

First, I don't think so.

Second, it doesn't matter.

Let's look at both statements.

First, I don't think people look down on gifts of *money* because money is such a highly charged symbol in our world. People scramble, fight, work, worry and die for money. They know its value. When most people receive it, they welcome it. Some people will grumble about the money not being enough, but that's their belief in lack and limitation. In general, give money and people will know you gave them something of real value.

Second, I don't think it matters what they think about the money or what they do with it. You're giving the money to activate your own heart.

My friend Bob Proctor, author of the book *You Were Born Rich*, once told me, "I don't care what they do with the money. They can take it out and burn it for all I care. I'm giving it for me."

And that's the point. While you want your gift to be received and appreciated, what you're really doing when you give it is awakening your own spirit and activating a spiritual law.

I remember giving a friend of mine a treasured copy of the now-legendary book, *The Robert Collier Letter Book*. The book is extremely rare, highly valued, and worth a lot of money.

My friend was at my house and said he had been looking for the book for years. I had an extra copy and just handed it to him. His eyes popped wide. He was stunned. He couldn't believe it, and he couldn't stop thanking me.

That was also the last time I saw my friend.

Did he not appreciate the gift?

Maybe.

Was it too much for him to receive as a gift?

Maybe.

Would I give it to him if I had to do it all over again?

In a heartbeat.

Giving that gift to him made *me* feel great.

Here's another example.

Some twenty-five years ago I was reading books and listening to tapes by Barry Neil Kaufman, founder of The Option Institute. I had little money at the time and found it hard to part with what I had. But I wanted to give something to show my support for Barry. So I sent him five dollars. It was a big deal for me, and I hoped it would somehow add to whatever others were sending to Barry.

Then, in 1985, I went to The Option Institute and studied with Barry, or "Bears," as his friends call him. On the last night of my stay there, we had a public Gratitude Night. Everyone who had been to the Institute that week gathered in a room, sat in a circle and took turns saying what we had been thankful for. This lasted *three hours.*

You can't imagine the energy in a room of thirty people thanking each other for three hours for all they had received. It was phenomenal. I still vividly recall that night.

When Bears took a moment to speak, he singled me out. He acknowledged me for my letters to him, for my support—and for the five dollars I had sent him many months earlier.

I was stunned.

While it had felt great to help Bears in a small way, I realized he had felt great to receive it. It was a beautiful win-win.

Remember, how you feel as you give is the key.

If the other person feels the joy, too—as Bears did with my gift—it's further reason to celebrate and feel happy.

And if the other person says little and maybe even drops out of your life—as my friend with the priceless book—allow it.

Again, how *you* feel as you give is the key.

"Money-giving is a very good criterion of a person's mental health. Generous people are rarely mentally ill people."

—Dr. Karl A. Menninger

47 Limiting Beliefs About Money –
And How to Release Them Right Now

By Mandy Evans

I've known Mandy Evans for about twenty years. She is a remarkable belief-clearing counselor. I asked her to compile a list of the most common negative or limiting beliefs about money that she could find. I also asked her to tell us how to remove them. The reason for my request is sometimes people give but have belief-blocks keeping them from receiving. Clear the blocks and the prosperity comes. The following article by Mandy offers a truly brilliant way out of the maze of limiting beliefs about money.

What you believe about money will play a greater role in your level of prosperity and in your enjoyment of that prosperity than most people imagine.

In fact, most people do not imagine the role beliefs play in their financial success or lack of it. Most people never even think about their beliefs. We just act on them.

I have been collecting examples of self-defeating beliefs like squirrels collect nuts for the winter for a long time. Here are some real beliefs about money from real people in real workshops and classes. These beliefs cut off the inflow of money into countless lives – or slowed it to a trickle. Some of them are familiar and some are so unique that they seem strange. Sometimes the same belief can be life-expanding for one person and life-extinguishing for another. Read through this list and see if you identify with any of the beliefs.

1. Money is the root of all evil. (The actual quote is "The love of money is the root of all evil.")

2. If I am successful people will hate me.

3. If I make a million dollars, I might lose it and then I would feel stupid and hate myself forever.

4. There is not enough money to go around.

5. If I have a little more than I need to get by, someone else has to go without.

6. If I have a lot more than I need to get by, lots of people will have to go without.

7. It is better to take less than to be responsible for someone else's hardship.

8. Democrats punish the rich.

9. Republicans punish the poor.

10. If I make a lot of money, I will be betraying my father who never made much money.

11. The rich get richer.

12. The poor get poorer.

13. I am smart and talented; I should get more!

14. You should always use money well.

15. Money is hard to deal with.

16. Money is hard to get.

17. You have to work hard to get it.

18. To save money you have to do without things.

19. Time is money.

20. I can't have money and free time.

21. Money is not spiritual.

22. You have to do lots of things you don't like in order to have money.

23. I do not have enough to share or give away.

24. Accepting money obligates me.

25. It is better to take less than my due and be free from sticky situations.

26. To be a valuable person I have to work more for less money than other people do.

27. Having money stops you from being happy.

28. Money spoils you.

29. I will never have enough.

30. If I don't feel bad about past mistakes and afraid about the future I will make the same mistakes again. (From an investment broker)

31. It's best if I just want enough to get by.

32. You get what you deserve.

33. Being super-conscious about every single penny is the good – the right – thing to do.

34. Never buy anything that you don't need.

35. If you were a smart woman you would be supporting yourself easily by now.

36. If you were a smart and cute woman you would have married someone with money by now.

37. I always rent; owning a house would be too scary.

38. I would never feel secure if I had to be responsible for much more than a hammock.

39. I have to own my own home to feel secure – unless I had at least maybe a yacht. If I buy something that breaks, I'm stupid.

40. Worrying about money is tacky.

41. Daddy will like me better if I don't spend much.

42. I want to have a lot of money when I get old, then people will be nice to me.

43. I never want people to know I have so much money because people are really mean to rich people.

44. If I get paid a lot people will find out that I am a fraud.

45. Daddy will love me lots more if I don't spend much.

46. Everybody wants more; when it comes to money, less is better.

47. There's somebody else inside me that spends all of my money.

If you identify with any of these beliefs, go though them one by one and answer these three questions about each belief.

- Why do I believe that?
- Is it true?
- What might I be concerned would happen if I did *not* believe that?

By asking those three probing questions of any belief, you can discharge it—and become free to go for your desires.

You'll also be free to give—as well as to receive.

Go ahead and work through those beliefs right now.

Mandy Evans has taught thousands of people how to become freer, more creative, and much happier by changing the beliefs that keep them stuck, limit them, and cause emotional pain. Her books "TRAVELLING FREE: How to Recover From the Past" and "Emotional Options" drew endorsements from Deepak Chopra, Bernie Siegel, John Gray and me. Visit www.mandyevans.com Order her books from www.amazon.com or call 800-431-1579.

"One of the reasons many people do not have money is that they are silently or openly condemning it."

—Joseph Murphy, *How To Attract Money*

Enlightenment-by-Email, or, How to Make Your Great TUT Come True

Mike Dooley didn't know what he was going to do. He quit his job at Price Waterhouse. He left the company, his security, and his home. He went to Orlando and sat there, lost, confused, waiting for direction. None came.

Meanwhile, his brother was making some money from royalties on a few t-shirts he had designed. So Mike, his brother, and later their mother, went into the T-shirt business. They called their business TUT, for Totally Unique T-shirts. Everyone from Disney to Macy's bought and sold them. Within ten years they sold more than one million shirts. Life was good.

As the market began to change, and major buyers began to make their own T-shirts, the family decided to stop business. The artistic brother began a career as an actor and improv comic. The enterprising mother, who had already written two books, began a full-time career as a writer. Mike decided to buy out the family business—which by that time had come to be known as "Totally Unique Thoughts"—and run it himself.

"Our most popular T-shirts had always been the ones with inspiring or spiritual sayings written on them," Mike told me over the phone one day. "So I decided to offer a Monday Morning Motivator by e-mail to our loyal list of followers."

The Monday memos were usually poems. And his small band of followers at the time amounted to 1,000 names. Instead of writing to these people with an opening that said, "Dear loyal T-shirt customer...," Mike decided on a more unique approach.

"I created an Adventurer's Club and invited them to be a member for the sum of only $36 a year," Mike explained. "They would get weekly and even daily messages from me, all of an inspiring, motivational and/or spiritual nature."

Did it work?

"No. Almost no one paid for it. So I naturally decided to offer it for free, knowing I would somehow figure out how to make money from it down the road."

Mike's Monday Morning Memos caught on. People loved the inspiring weekly poetry. Eventually he gathered the courage to add his own insightful commentaries that would accompany each poem. His subscriber base grew to 3,000 names.

"About this time I had a friend of mine who was making $15,000 every month from banner ads on his e-cards," says Mike. "So I put all my energy into making free e-cards that people could sponsor click-through ads on. I used the old T-shirt art I had and added some commentary to make the e-cards unique."

But that didn't work out, either.

"Within six months advertisers quit taking ads on e-cards. My friend stopped making $15,000 a month. I never made more than $100 from my e-cards. But I'm still glad I did them."

Why is he glad?

"They have become a viral marketing campaign," Mike explains. "People send them to others and suddenly my website is known to potentially millions of people. Those e-cards are still a popular feature on my website."

Around this time—in 2001—Mike decided to take the biggest leap of faith of all.

"I recorded 12 audiotapes, packaged them, and called them *Infinite Possibilities: The Art of Living Your Dreams*. They are a combination of my weekly e-memos, old talks I had given, and entirely fresh material."

That tape set became a turning point for Mike's online business.

"People would get an e-card from someone, see a link at the bottom for my tapes, and make an impulse buy right then and there."

Mike sells 40 to 60 tape sets every month, at a retail price of $125 for either cassettes or CDs.

While he's never asked for a single testimonial for his tapes, he has at this point collected an overwhelming amount of them. You can see them at http://www.tut.com/auwc.htm

Here are three quick ones:

"Riveting. Inspiring. Even miraculous. Rarely have I heard such wisdom, such mind-stretching beauty, such practical inspiration and proven advice."

"I was blown away! I squealed with delight!"

"I'm listening to the tapes repeatedly...EXCELLENT material, endless new perspectives, spin-offs...your words have set me in motion!"

While Mike has added a daily e-memo to his weekly ones, he has never advertised, done any publicity, or implemented any marketing. His tape sales come from word-of-mouth sharing. His database is currently 5,000 hot names, and growing. He plans to use pay-per-click services to build his database. Next he'll focus on his affiliate program, which he just added to his site.

In short, Mike went from a company drop-out with no mission to a man with a giant mission. And he uses the Internet as his primary vehicle to help people go for their dreams. His main marketing tool is his "Enlightenment-by-E-mail" daily and weekly inspiring messages, which continue to be free.

What's his advice for building a successful business and making your own TUT—totally unique thoughts—come true?

"As clearly as possible define the end result of what you want in emotional terms," he advises. "Get into that emotion now, even before you start working for the dream or even quitting your job. Having the end result firmly in mind now will help you weather any setbacks that may occur later."

"And don't worry about how you will get to that end result," he adds. "There are a million ways to achieve fame or wealth, or whatever you want. Don't tie the hands of the universe by thinking it has to come in one certain way. The universe has 'Infinite Possibilities' at its beck and call. Trust it."

Finally, I asked Mike if he would offer a "totally unique thought" specifically for you, the reader of this book. Here's what he sent:

"Success in the world, business or otherwise, is far more a function of how well you engage the Universe and its magic, than it is of how well you manipulate the time and space around you. This is every tycoon's secret – whether they know it or not.

"Your job is NOT to out-maneuver the competition, to play into the hands of future clients and customers, or to reinvent the wheel. Your job is to define your dream, to imagine the end result, and to move with your hunches and instincts – that's it. The rest will automatically and effortlessly fall into place…a brilliant marketing strategy, the best "location," the "clutch" idea, and perfect timing between them. The Universe is ALIVE in the unseen, and active in all of your affairs. Learn how to use it."

And here's another very relevant quote from Mike:

"GIVING tells the Universe that you believe YOU are provided for. For even as you empty your purse you fear not, demonstrating faith that you will remain whole, that your coffers will be replenished, and that your love for whomever you gave, is what's most important. Verily, as you believe these things to be true, you will experience such truths, and abundance shall be showered upon you as if the heavens had opened up."

You'll note that a large degree of Mike's success came from giving—he gave away (and still gives away) e-cards, and he still writes and gives away his inspiring daily and weekly memos.

Total sales, plus speaking fees, and revenues from new books in the mill (*Notes from the Universe, Totally Unique Thoughts, More Reminders Of Life's Everyday Magic*, etc,) should top $250,000 this year, and Mike projects $1,000,000 in 2004!

Mike says, "None of this would have happened if I hadn't offered all my mailings, and club membership for free, though at the time I had no idea of where it would take me, nor of how I would eventually profit. It just felt right, people were grateful, and I was loving my 'job.'

"Sometimes the Universe doesn't always respond in kind, or by throwing dollars at you, but instead, it returns to you confidence, dreams, and inspiration...which is even better than bucks, because it's like learning to fish (as opposed to being given a fish). You then know how to go get more."

How Giving Led to $1,500,000

By John Milton Fogg

Lots of authors take custody of the "best-seller" claim for their book. Yeah, well...it may be a best-seller at the "Ain't Words Cool" book store in their own home town, but...It's a whole other thing to be able to say that a book has sold a million copies!

That's just what John Milton Fogg can claim for his book "The Greatest Networker in the World." How did he do that? John's answer is...

I gave the book away.

I wrote *The Greatest Networker...*in 1992. At the time I was the owner/editor of a publication named *Upline*, that served men and women in the network marketing profession. At that time, we probably had a couple of thousand subscribers at most.

I didn't have the money for the first-print run. A friend and mentor of mine in the business, Tom "Big Al" Schreiter, suggested I "pre-sell" the books to people who could sell them to others: book wholesalers, vendors to network marketers, people who had magazines or catalogs which sold books, tapes and tools. Tom told me to make a great low-price deal to these folks so they could make more money. That would pay for the printing, make a profit for myself and generate the money to print more books. Tom bought 1000 copies at $3 each.

I asked him how he was going to sell those books. He told me he wasn't. He was going to *give them away.*

That got my attention, so I asked, "Why?"

Tom explained he was going to "seed" the market. He figured people would like or love the book, and they'd come back and buy more to give or sell to other people. And, it would create word-of-mouth advertising for the book, which meant more sales for him (and me).

Tom also explained the idea of a "value-added" premium to me: He'd make an offer of one of his products to his people and give *The Greatest Networker*...away free as an incentive to buy. People would get a $10 value, which Tom only paid $3 for.

Good deal for him – helped him sell more of his products.

Good deal for them – they got a free gift, felt great and were more inclined to buy his offer.

I don't know how many of my books Tom sold over the years. I do know he made his investment back and them some – lots of some.

I knew a great idea when I saw one, so I started giving *The Greatest Networker*...away with every single subscription to *Upline.*

My subscribers got a free gift and were more likely to buy the magazine to begin with. I got my book being read by the best possible people who could spread the word and help me sell more.

When the Internet came along, I put *The Greatest Networker...* up on our website and gave it away there, too.

Over the years I probably gave away 40,000-plus copies of my book. The cost of that was, say, $50,000. So one way to look at it was I gave away $50,000.

But I earned a buck a book royalty on all the copies of *The Greatest Networker in the World* that were sold. That doesn't include any "extra" money I earned from the wholesale or retail sales when people bought the book.

Do the math.

My guess would be all-in-all that's $1.5 million of net profit to me.

All because I gave my book away.

Here's yet another true story about the power of giving:

Do you know who Seth Godin is? (He's the *other* Internet Marketing guru besides Joe.) :-) Seth wrote *The Idea Virus*. That book started a revolution. Seth gave it away on-line. People told him he was crazy. More than a million and a-half of Seth's e-books are out there. AND, after he gave it away for free, he printed up a hard-cover edition for $45 and made a fortune selling that! Go figure.

I had the fascinating privilege of interviewing Seth Godin for *Networking Times* magazine. He told me the following "Giving-Marketing" story and it just blew me away. This is utterly brilliant!

Seth knows a great folksinger who does music for kids. She has five CDs and she sells them on her own. Now, Seth doesn't do consulting any more, but this lady is a personal friend, so when she asked if he had any ideas on how she could sell more of her CDs, Mr. *Permission Marketing* (he wrote that book, too) complied.

Seth asked how much she sold her CDs for. She told him $15. Seth asked how much one cost her to produce and package. She told him 80 cents. So Seth said…

"Look, every time someone buys one CD, send them two. Nobody has any use for a second CD, because it's the same music. What are they going to do? They're going to give it away, probably as a present. One of these kids gives one of these CDs to another kid as a birthday present and they're likely to buy two, three or four more, because the parents get tired of hearing the same songs over and over again."

Like I said, "Brilliant." Each one of those give-away CDs that results in just one additional sale nets the folksinger $14.20. And as Seth pointed out, parents will probably buy two or three more, perhaps all five. And each time they do, they get an extra one free, that they turn around and give to a friend saying, "This is great. Little Harry will really love this."

Oh, that lady folksinger doubled, then tripled her business with that CD she gave away.

John Milton Fogg's website is at:
http://www.GreatestNetworker.com/is/jmf

A Law That Never Fails

By Dr. Robert Anthony

Two years ago I received an email from a friend that said, "I just came across a website that has a quote from one of your books right on the front page."

I checked it out and sure enough, there was a quote from my book, *Advanced Formula For Total Success,* prominently featured on the main page.

After looking over the website I was impressed with the service the owner was offering. I contacted him and told him so. In addition to the quote, I offered to write a short article endorsing his service. He couldn't believe I would do this for him without compensation.

My intention was to support him and help him to succeed. It never even occurred to me to ask for anything in return. I knew that the universe would take care of any "compensation."

As a result of my endorsement I found out that during the following year he had increased his sales significantly. During that time we never kept in contact and truthfully I had forgotten all about it.

A little over a year later I received an email from him that said, "Someone contacted me because they saw your endorsement on my website and said they wanted to get in touch with you. He says it is very important. Do you want me to give him your personal email address?"

Strangely enough I had no hesitation and said, "Yes, have him contact me."

This is the only communication I had with the website owner since I helped him over a year ago.

I followed up and contacted the man who wrote to him. That one contact changed my life.

As it turned out, this individual became a close friend as well as my new business manager and marketer. As a result, with his help, my business increased over 500%!

All this from giving freely to someone without asking for something in return. This was a clear and direct result of the Law of Reciprocation (giving/receiving) in action.

A law that NEVER fails.

Dr. Robert Anthony is the author of several best-selling books. See his website at www.drrobertanthony.com

Giving Really Does Lead
To Receiving

By Bob Burg

Whenever I speak on the topic of Networking, I always make sure to provide my definition of what the term "Networking" means to me.

By and large, the very concept is misunderstood and carries with it a somewhat negative preconceived notion (i.e., shove as many business cards into people's faces as you can while telling them all about yourself and your products or services while attending a one-hour business/social mixer).

I define Networking as "The cultivating of mutually beneficial, *give* and take, win/win relationships."

As you can see, the emphasis is on the "give" part.

"But wait," the person asks, "Isn't that just Pollyanna-type thinking that doesn't work in the real world?"

Not at all. Giving works.

Let me say it again. Giving works!

And there's nothing "Pollyanna" about it. Giving works both from a practical, as well as spiritual side. Let's look though, at just the practical side.

What I call "The Golden Rule" of Networking is, "All things being equal, people will do business with, and refer business to, those people they know, like and trust."

When we give to – or do something for – someone, we take an important step toward causing those "know, like and trust" feelings toward us in that other person. I've often said that the best way to get business and get referrals is to first give business and give referrals.

Why? Because when someone knows you care about them enough to send business their way, they feel good about you. No, they feel *great* about you, and desire to give back to you.

Of course, it doesn't have to be actual business that you give. It could be information, whether that information is something that would help them in regard to their business, personal, social, or recreational lives.

Perhaps you suggested a book (or bought them that book) that you know would be of true value to that person.

Maybe you knew their son or daughter was looking for work at a certain company and, knowing someone there who knew the personnel director, you made a call and put in the kind word that helped ensure employment.

It really doesn't matter. Allow me, if you will, to share one example from my personal life. This took place several years after I had begun speaking professionally. There was one corporate client in particular – one with many divisions – I had been trying to "land." However, I could not seem to even get a foot in the door. Not only that, I couldn't even find the door to try and stick my foot in.

It happened that at a Speakers' convention I met a man who had been speaking professionally for quite a while. I struck up a friendship with him and his family and looked forward to seeing them at various events.

During that time, despite the fact that I knew he was quite successful, I never asked him for anything. I did, however, help him as much as I could. Several times, when I was already booked for an engagement on a certain date, I would refer him to the person from the company who had called me.

Having articles published fairly often in magazines, I would refer him as a contributor to the editor. This was appreciated by all parties, of course, and didn't take anything from me in any way. That's one of the great things about giving; it helps everyone and hurts no one.

It was only a couple of years after meeting him that I found out, through a third party, that the client I had been unsuccessfully seeking, was a major client of this speaker friend of mine.

Now, I probably could have come right out and asked him for help but I didn't feel that would be quite right. I didn't want him to feel that because I had gone out of my way for him that he "owed" me anything. I did feel comfortable, however, asking for his advice on how I might myself best pursue them.

I said to him, "I know this is a huge client of yours and am not in any way asking for you to make a connection for me. I'd love to know, though, how would be the best way for me to contact the person myself to at least let them know who I am and how I could help them, so that I get the opportunity to establish and develop a relationship?"

Well, to make a long story end, he would have none of that.

He said, "I'll have the guy who's my main contact call you."

And he did.

And that client, together will all the spin-off engagements I've had wetting that company's umbrella over the years has accounted for several million dollars in sales.

And that was not the first, and certainly not the only time, that giving first has literally paid big financial dividends. It's the way I run my business; it's the way I run my life.

Giving first works.

There is a major caution here, however: You cannot give with the *expectation* of direct reciprocation or, for that matter, *any* reciprocation.

This won't work if you are thinking, "Okay, what is he or she going to do for me?"

Not that you might not get something in return. But that something will more than likely be a one-time something, done out of obligation, and not inspiring the "know you, like you, and trust you" feelings toward you from that other person that will elicit this person desiring to see you successful.

No, give because it's the right thing, without the expectation of direct reciprocation, and you'll find this principle to be one of the truest of universal truths.

Bob Burg speaks internationally on the topics of "Business Networking" and "Positive Persuasion Skills." His books "Endless Referrals" and "Winning Without Intimidation" have each sold over 100,000 copies. To subscribe to Bob's free weekly email newsletter, visit www.burg.com

"Love must be the guiding principle in all our giving."
—James A. Decker, *Magnificent Decision*

Giving and Receiving: The Fine Print No One Told You About

By John Zappa

Much has been written about the universal law of giving and receiving, but I have discovered in my dealings with others that there is often a great deal of misunderstanding about how to apply the principle.

The general notion is that the more you give, the more you get. As you sow, so shall you reap. That's all well and good, but I believe the misunderstanding of this wonderful secret could be easily cleared up with a simple corollary to the law of giving. The corollary is that it's not what you do but why you do it. Intention and motivation are everything.

What this means is that you should only give if you are giving for the pure joy of giving. If you give because you expect to get, you are defeating the purpose. The universe is not so easily fooled. Giving with the motive of getting is actually an affirmation of lack. Saying that you have to get because you have just given is saying to the world "I don't have enough." Your belief will soon be proven correct. The energy vibration of lack will only attract more lack.

Again, as you sow, so shall you reap.

Many people I know give grudgingly or feel deprived after they have made a gift of time or money. If you give out of a feeling of obligation or a sense of sacrifice, the underlying feeling is one of lack. Dressing up a feeling of lack under a mask of generosity will only lead to disappointment. It's not what you do but why you do it.

Don't waste your time by giving with the expectation of getting a return on your investment. God is not a share of stock that you trade on the NASDAQ (ticker symbol GODD). "If I give, I'd better get something back or else." Such thinking originates from a position of "there's not enough."

While some people give with ulterior motives, there are others of us who rarely give at all because of the belief, "I can't afford it." Henry Ford often said that there are two kinds of people...Those that think they can and those that think they can't; and they're both right. Your beliefs create your experience every time.

So much for the ways NOT to give. What to do instead?

My personal experience suggests waiting until you are in flow with life. We all have mood swings. Sometimes we feel good, and sometimes we feel bad. When you happen to catch yourself feeling good, seize that opportunity to give out of a sense of sharing the abundance that is already yours.

By being grateful for whatever you currently have, it is much easier to pass some of your good fortune onto someone else. In those moments, you get the sense that there is more where that came from.

My first experience with true giving, at least in recent memory, occurred during a relapse of cancer several years ago. Once I got over the initial shock of the diagnosis, spiritual aspects within me started to awaken and I began to count my blessings.

After several months of chemotherapy, I had the opportunity to visit New York City during the Christmas holiday season. My doctor had decided to give me a few weeks off from chemotherapy to enjoy the holidays, and a mini-vacation was just what I needed. The Christmas lights in NYC, the crisp winter air, and the fact that I was still alive put me in good spirits. I was feeling abundant and grateful.

One evening on the way to dinner with my wife and my brother, a homeless man outside the restaurant we had selected asked me if I could spare a dollar. I was feeling great, and I gave him $20 instead. This in turn made him feel great, and it made me feel even better that I had made his day. The important subtlety for me was that I had waited for my wife and my brother to go inside the restaurant before I gave him the money. I wanted the act to be anonymous, and I didn't want anyone questioning the wisdom of giving away a $20 bill while I was on medical leave with a very limited income. If I had to defend or justify my actions to anyone else, it would have taken away the joy and spontaneity of the moment.

At that point, I did not know what the future had in store for me, but in that instant things were perfect. I was feeling good, and I didn't want anyone else to ruin the feeling of that moment by telling me to be sensible. Waiting until no one was looking to give this man some money seemed like the best means to that end.

It was a win-win situation. The guy felt great, and I continued to feel great the rest of the evening. It was my secret. I was feeling prosperous for no apparent reason, and I made someone else feel prosperous by giving him 20 times more than he had asked for or expected. I happened to be in the flow of life in that moment, and it was a perfect time to give.

Over the next few months, my supposedly "fixed" disability payments somehow increased by 20%. I don't know how or why, and I certainly didn't ask.

I did not know about the law of giving and receiving at that time in my life. I was just acting on pure impulse. It was only after I began my spiritual studies that I came across this principle. With my new understanding and the benefit of hindsight, I began to see the connection.

The most important aspect of this principle to me, and it bears repeating, is to remember that it is not what you do but why you do it. If you are having a bad day, or you are in a negative frame of mind, don't give just because you think you are supposed to. There is no extra credit for God, and it won't benefit you or the other person under those conditions.

Instead, wait until you are having a particularly good day and are feeling great. Then give while you are in that state, and observe what happens. If you find yourself doing mathematical calculations to decide how much you can afford to give or worry over what others think is sensible, don't bother. You've lost the feeling.

Wait until you're back in the flow and just choose an amount based on your first impulse. Go with whatever amount makes you feel good and that won't cause you to feel poorer because there is that much less in your wallet or bank account.

This universal law may take only a moment to understand, but it can take a lifetime to master. But just because you haven't mastered it does not mean that you can't have fun practicing. Give it a try, and let your own experience be the judge.

John Zappa is a publicity consultant in Austin, Texas. As a refugee from Corporate America, he now chooses to invent his own work.

How to Get What You Want

By Susie and Otto Collins

It seems like such a strange concept, but when you give away what you want—you really do get more of it.

We're living proof. And here's why...

We have an incredible relationship filled with lots of love, passion and a deep connection with each other and with our creator.

Our relationships weren't always like this. In fact our previous relationships were in many ways a mirror for what we didn't want.

Before getting together, totally independent of each other, we each decided we were willing to do whatever was necessary to create the relationship of our dreams.

Out of our passion to have this incredible relationship, we read every book, went to every seminar, listened to every tape and spent countless hours talking about and discussing relationships trying to figuring out what it takes to create the relationship of our dreams.

So what did we do next?

We began giving love away.

Out of our own passion for love, connection and having a great relationship—we began sharing with others what we had discovered.

As a result of our desire to "give love away" and share with others what we've learned about love, relationships and happiness, not only has our own relationship grown deeper and more connected but our bank account has grown as well.

People started asking us what we did to create such a great relationship.

So in 1999 we started an online newsletter on relationships and personal growth.

We simply shared tips and ideas we used to create a great relationship.

In other words we gave away what we most wanted: Love.

Now, almost 20,000 people get our free weekly Relationship Gold newsletter.

We've also written three books on relationships including *Communication Magic, Should You Stay or Should You Go?* and *Creating Relationship Magic*. We have two others planned.

We're not counselors or therapists. We simply share from our hearts and lives what we know about love and relationships that we wish we'd known years ago.

What we have is so great that we want others to know how they can have it too.

We have discovered that just like money, there is an abundance of love that is there wanting to be tapped into.

We just have to be willing to be open to it.

What we wanted more than anything else was a deep, connected, loving relationship.

We are now happy to say that with each other we have the kind of relationship that we want.

As a result of "giving love away"—we're not only getting love back—but, now we're being rewarded with financial abundance as well.

This is an abundant universe we live in.

Give, Give, Give.

There will be more where that came from.

Susie and Otto Collins are Relationship Coaches, Authors and married Life Partners from Ohio. For more info on their books, tapes, seminars or to sign up for their free weekly Relationship Gold online newsletter, visit their websites at http://www.collinspartners.com or http://www.RelationshipGold.com

What to Give When You Don't Have Any Money

By Christopher Guerriero

About two years ago, although I had several high-income businesses, I had very little personal income from those businesses – but I still felt a passion for giving – I just had nothing to give (or so I thought).

During the months that I stopped tithing (giving), I found that things got even harder – in fact – even proven marketing campaigns that my company had run many times in the past stopped pulling in revenue. At times I felt like there was a dark cloud following me.

I knew from years of experience that the more I gave, the more I would receive in return, but again, I had little to give (financially) and several businesses to support, along with all the families of the employees that went along with each of those businesses.

What I learned in those early days was that my giving didn't necessarily have to come from my bank account. And that during the lean years, I needn't give money. *I just had to keep "giving"* to help set up for all the "receiving" that was in store for me in later years.

I learned that when I stopped giving, I literally 'clogged up' all the good that God had in store for me. So I began giving what I did have – time, prayers, and lots of help to those who needed my specialized help.

When I look back, I see those lean years as a test to see if I could learn how to give even when it seemed to hurt to do so. I also look back and thank God for that experience and for what it taught me—which was—to never stop giving. I can change the form of my tithing, I can even change the amount of my tithing, but I will never stop tithing.

I now tithe as much as I can financially, then I make up the difference in some other category. I always financially tithe first, because to reach the goals I have in life I need a lot of money to circulate through me and my businesses.

It's been my experience that giving is the secret to keeping money, success, health, love and happiness circulating through your life.

Christopher Guerriero, Author of the best-selling book "Maximize Your Metabolism – Double your metabolism in 30 days or less!" See www.MaximizeYourMetabolism.com

It Took Me 30 Years to
Learn This Secret

By Richard Webster

I have always given, but funnily enough, I gave out of fear.

If someone asked me for money, I would always put my hand in my pocket. If they didn't ask, I would walk past without offering anything.

My thinking was that if someone asked, I had a choice of saying "yes" or "no." If I gave them money, it meant I would always have money. If I said "no," I was subconsciously attracting a lack of money.

So it was the fear of having a lack of money that made me give. Of course, although I was giving, it was always small amounts.

The Richard Webster Popular Fiction Award changed my life. It developed from a slightly boozy lunch I had with some writer friends. We were bemoaning the fact that authors of popular fiction found it hard to get published and receive any recognition. Writers of literary fiction received grants and other handouts to get their work published, but commercial writers received nothing. I announced that I'd launch an award, with a prize of $1,000. My friends laughed, and the conversation went to other things. However, the thought stayed with me, and eventually I decided to go ahead with it. I must admit my motives were selfish. I thought that having an award with my name on it would increase my name and reputation, and that might help book sales.

I found a publisher who was prepared to publish the winning entry, and two years ago we launched it. I increased the first prize to $5,000, and added a second prize of $1,000. This seemed like a huge amount of money to give away.

To my pleasure, the award did increase my exposure, and I gave dozens of newspaper articles and radio interviews. I don't think any author has ever sponsored an award for other authors before, and this made it newsworthy. I felt good about doing it, but didn't expect any other benefits.

However, to my amazement, this award seemed to open a floodgate of money.

My book sales increased.

The foreign language rights sales to my books multiplied, and I received paid offers to speak all around the world.

My income, which comes entirely from my books, more than doubled in the first twelve months.

Naturally, I'm much more generous now than I used to be. I love giving money away. And the more I give away, the better off I become.

I wish I'd learned this secret thirty years ago.

Richard Webster lives in New Zealand and has written numerous books, including "Is Your Pet Psychic?" See his websites at www.psychic.co.nz and www.richardwebster.co.nz

"Act wealthy. Talk prosperously. Be a free avenue through which riches may pass to all. The world needs to learn the spiritual science of wealth, and your home can be a classroom."

—Annie Rix Militz, *Both Riches and Honor*

How Giving and "Swiping" Led to Passive Income

By Larry Dotson

It was back in September, 2001 when I completed an e-book titled *The Hypnotic Writer's Swipe File*. The term 'swipe file' was coined by copywriters who collected sales generating words and phrases throughout their careers to model and use in their own sales letters.

My problem was I wasn't sure how I was going to market the e-book. I really didn't have a targeted customer base at the time. So I decided to ask Joe Vitale if he would co-author the book with me for a share of the profits. I was willing to give him authorship credit and share the profits with him, too.

I knew that Joe's series of "hypnotic" e-books was already branded and famous. When you think of hypnotic writing, copywriting, and marketing, you think of Joe Vitale, 'The World's First Hypnotic Writer and Marketer.'

Joe agreed. He wrote a truly hypnotic introduction to the book, added a lot of his own material to what I had already compiled, and we released our book later that same year.

The rest is history. Since that first e-book, Joe and I have co-authored 7 more hypnotic e-books.

And when Joe was planning to write an e-book on "Hypnotic Stories" by himself—which he was obviously capable of doing—he asked me if I wanted to be the co-author of it. He didn't have to do that. But because I gave to him, he felt like giving to me. That end result was a beautiful e-book called *Hypnotic Selling Stories*.

By giving to Joe, and him giving back to me, we both received. We make a good amount of money every month from our e-books, and we developed a strong online friendship and solid business relationship. To this date, we still haven't met in person, or even talked by phone. All of our co-authoring has been done by e-mail only.

And it all started from giving.

Larry Dotson is the co-author of several books with me.
See http://www.HypnoticWritingSwipeFile.com

How Giving Made A Book
A #1 Best-Seller

By Mike Litman

Over the course of a year, I worked to heap as much life-changing value and content on my newsletter readers: Information that would literally blow them away from what they were compared to getting from other ezines on the Internet.

Each week, I'd ask these questions, "How can I go the extra mile for my valued readers?" and "How can I give them more than they'd ever expect?"

My newsletter subscribers grew to love me and my work. I was continuously giving them all I could.

In the middle of 2001, I wrote a book. A host of book publishers mocked us saying, "No one will read your book *Conversations with Millionaires*. No one wants to read your actual conversations from your little radio show." So we were left to go down this road alone.

My co-author, Jason Oman, and I were first-time authors, self-publishing a book. We didn't know what to do. But we knew we had a list of loyal followers. All we had to do is ask for their help.

What the publishers didn't get is that we had *thousands* of people who were ready to help us because of how we first went the extra mile and served them.

That's the power of what I call *Loverage*.

On January 18, 2002, 76 days after the book's release, without spending money on advertising, public relations and without public speaking, we knocked John Grisham off the top spot at Amazon.com and claimed it!

We had ourselves a #1 best-selling book.

Also, it brought in over $31,070 in sales!

The power of giving leads to the fountain of receiving.

We've received an abundance of money, new friends, and a 'path' that helps many. Also, the book has already been translated into three languages.

Since then this 'little book that could' has been touching the lives of tens of thousands of people, all because when you give without expecting anything in return, you get more then you could ever want. As you sow, so shall you reap.

When 'they' mock you because you desire to serve and give, you think about the story of *Conversations with Millionaires*.

Mike Litman is the co-author of the #1 Best-Selling book "Conversations with Millionaires."
http://www.mikelitman.com

The Principle of Giving and
The Hypnotic Interchange Phenomenon

By Allen D'Angelo

Many years ago I discovered the Principle of Giving almost by accident.

Initially, around 1994, I noticed that several business clients sent me markedly more referrals after I sent them a huge box of Godiva Chocolates as a thank-you for their business. I noticed that the clients who received chocolates referred around 40% more clients to me than the clients who did not receive my tasty gifts. Actually, in earlier years prior to my *chocolateering* endeavors most of my clients gave me "no referrals" whatsoever—and I might add, in those days quite regularly.

One day upon receiving a swarm of referrals I decided to deepen my commitment to giving. Initially, honestly, it was for self-serving reasons. I was simply blown away by what appeared to be a strong causal relationship between giving and receiving. At that time all I knew was that I had to learn more because I recognized a new, almost mysteriously powerful aspect of giving at work behind the scenes here.

For the first time I understood clearly that somehow in the vast scheme of life we are rewarded in direct proportion to the value we create for others. I had heard once that the secret to abundant wealth was in creating massive value for others. But, based on my newfound experiences, I was now discovering with renewed white heat fervor that the Principle of Giving was the "gold-rush flume-ride" to expedite that flow of wealth into my life.

My self-serving commitment to discover more about giving soon led to a way of life that I later realized would continue to fuel me much more spiritually than it ever would economically. Little did I realize that my seemingly rare flowering rose-like discovery would soon open up into an entire inner garden paradise for me.

I conducted several very powerful experiments on the subject of how giving leads to receiving. I made a deeper, less self-interested, but more self-enlightened commitment. It was out of my simple curiosity to see how I could change others' lives through profound value-sharing as a regular business and life practice.

I began giving more than merely chocolate candies—although Godiva certainly soothes the deepest recesses of my own soul. I gave valuable advice. There were bonus hours spent with clients, e-books, and article clippings sent to friends about their favorite hobbies. I gave as much as I could to those with whom I had a regular influence.

If someone crossed my pathway, I figured it was for a higher-causal purpose and I just shared the most appropriate level of value I could with that person. I did it everyday, one person at a time. I did it with my lists of exclusive business mastermind participants. I did it with my e-list recipients.

For me, it felt like magic. It flowed effortlessly. It transformed my soul. It replaced expensive marketing in my businesses. Best of all, my interior castle would soar into the highest heaven with each person whose life I had the privilege of touching.

Soon my hidden objective was to cause everyone I met to think of me as a value creator. My goal was to become a selfless abundant resource. You see, I had a hunch that if I focused more on opening the doorway of my heart to the needs of other people by giving, that this would cause the doorway of my recipients' hearts to open back up to me.

So acting on the Principle of Giving first induces openness in others. This is a powerful precursor for relationship-building—business, personal and otherwise.

I then discovered that as a value creator I must give sincerely, selflessly, abundantly, effortlessly, with absolutely no expectation of a direct immediate reward. I also realized that I must be balanced in giving in order to respect the true value of the gifts I gave. Gifts are not only reflections of us, but actual experiential portions of ourselves embodied in external expressions.

The same goes for you, too. Every gift that you give which has exceptional meaning and value for your recipient is actually a portion of yourself.

The gift is a part of you that reaches out, makes a connection point and creates a powerful relationship-building bond to your recipient.

The act of bestowing value on others exerts a positive supernatural influence upon any recipient who understands and values your gift.

Shortly after committing to the Principle of Giving as a philosophy of life, I began to notice the occurrence of quite a remarkable spin-off phenomenon occurring.

As a disciple of Joe Vitale's Hypnotic Mindset and Principles, I named my unique observation "the Hypnotic Interchange Phenomenon" because it describes a result of giving that is so subtle it flies under the radar of most people's conscious "rejection detection."

The Hypnotic Interchange Phenomenon is this:

The recipient of my valuable gift unknowingly enters into an implied equal psychological exchange with me instantly upon receiving what I give them.

That's right. By receiving what I had freely given them, my recipients were becoming programmed to look for every way possible to give something of equal value back to me. At times it would be through a kind word they said about me to a friend. Often it would be a referral to two or three other business partners.

Often I would contact someone to ask him or her if they received a gift I had sent to them, and they would usually overflow with gratitude. It was at those times I realized that my gifts were like planted seeds that would produce a good harvest in a very reasonable time.

It is vital to remind ourselves of the importance of giving something that has a true, high-perceived value for those you choose to lavish your gifts upon.

The psychology of human behavior is relatively timeless. Master philosophers of past centuries share incredible secrets about the Principle of Giving. Here is a small sample:

Eric Hoffer, of the 20th century, a profound U.S. philosopher, said, "Someone gives us all he has and we are his."

20th-Century German philosopher Walter Benjamin said, "Gifts must affect the receiver to the point of shock."

Jean de La Bruyere, 17th-century French writer, said, "Generosity lies less in giving much than in giving at the right moment."

6th-Century Chinese philosopher, Lao-Tsu, said, "The sage does not hoard. Having bestowed all he has on others, he has yet more. Having given all he has to others, he is richer still."

My most recent life work, over two years in the making, has expanded to spurring others to give extreme levels of value. I have been working hard to successfully funnel-influence my dearest friends who are famous writers and authors to give massive value through me.

These are people who have earned the right to be called rich and famous because they have sold millions of books using the Principle of Giving. They are profound master contributors in our modern world. Now they are freely sharing their secrets with you.

These master contributors include Joe Vitale (*Spiritual Marketing*), James Redfield (*The Celestine Prophecy*), Dick Bolles (*What Color Is Your Parachute?*), Dave Chilton (*The Wealthy Barber*), and many others.

In keeping with my commitment to becoming an extreme value creator, we are lavishing on anyone who visits http://www.TotalBookMarketing.com over $468 worth of valuable book publishing, e-book, and infopreneur marketing insights from masters who have made millions and have given away a lot. They include the best minds I have ever known or worked with in over 14 years of publishing, marketing and consulting.

Most of all, when you visit TotalBookMarketing.com you'll be encouraged, uplifted and overwhelmed to see that there are people who truly want to help others—who take action to give by putting the needs of others before their own needs. That alone is a testimony to giving—that it works and works well.

Interestingly, Joe Vitale was one of the very first friends to jump at the chance to contribute to "TotalBookMarketing.com." Joe is the greatest value creator I know—because he puts his heart into giving and he is always sharing all the value he's got.

Learn and do.

To see a great example of the Principle of Giving and the Hypnotic Interchange Phenomenon at work on the Internet, visit Allen's website at http://www.TotalBookMarketing.com.

"A gift with reservations is not a gift; it is a bribe. There is no promise of increase unless we give freely. Let go of the gift entirely. Recognize the universal scope of the law. Then the gift has a chance to go out and to come back multiplied. There is no telling how far the blessing may travel before it comes back. It is a beautiful and encouraging fact that the longer it is in returning, the more hands it is passing through and the more hearts it is blessing. All these hands and hearts add something to it in substance. It is increased all the more when it does return."

—Charles Fillmore, *Dynamics for Living*

Why Giving Is Really Hidden Selling

By Jo Han Mok

I was listening to Joe Vitale's best-selling Nightingale-Conant tape set, *The Power of Outrageous Marketing.*

Joe's hypnotic voice took me on a road trip.

"Who was the REAL beneficiary behind Bill Phillip's Body For Life Challenge?" he asked on the tapes.

It rang in my head and bounced off the walls of my brain like a rubber ball. I was in deep thought.

There is probably hardly a soul on this planet who has not seen those touching 'Before' and 'After' pictures and how the Body For Life Challenge has radically improved their lives. People were touched. People were motivated. Who did not want to undertake their own Body For Life Campaign and try to get trim?

But aside from implementing your 20-minute aerobic solution and grazing on 6 wholesome meals with nothing but quality fat-free, low-calorie food, what else do you need to accelerate your results?

Is it no surprise that EAS Supplements just POP right into your head immediately?

Bill Phillips was the CEO of EAS at that time. Now he's probably enjoying life on some tropical island somewhere, savoring his Myoplex Deluxe.

How much do you think EAS made from the Body For Life Challenge, and all its other sources of ancillary revenue like its *Muscle Media* magazine...which promotes more EAS supplements and success stories of Body For Life?

How would you feel if every success story credited their stunning success to proper supplementation of EAS products and they would never have done it without the help of EAS?

Would you want to run out to your friendly neighborhood GNC to buy a truckload of that stuff?

"Who was the REAL beneficiary behind Bill Phillip's Body For Life Challenge?"

You guess.

Yet on the surface, Bill Phillips gave hope to overweight people and changed the life of hundreds of thousands, and reaffirmed people, that they could do it, too!! And of course, the unseen bracket after that statement would imply (if they used EAS Supplements).

It stirred within me a stunning revelation of the REAL key to unlocking the secret of wealth and abundance.

Giving is really *hidden selling*!!

The truth about selling is, if you're gonna sell something, you'll encounter resistance. Doesn't matter if you're a Zig Ziglar or not. Even Zig Ziglar could not achieve a 100% sales closure rate.

But if you want to GIVE something, guess how much resistance you'll encounter?

Zero. Zilch. Nada.

Not only will you NOT meet any resistance, but chances are people will RUSH to GRAB your gift with open arms. They cannot help but love you and think good things of you when you give them something.

When I started out writing copy I offered to write for FREE. I put in 10,000% of myself in these 'free' services.

Were people impressed? You bet. Did they like me? How could they not? I delivered everything for free.

How would you think my 'free' clients would feel about me when they start gaining a lifetime of profits from a sales letter I wrote for them—for free?

If all I asked for was just a testimonial for my services rendered, what kind of testimonial would they write for me?

Would they have any problems writing me a raving testimonial?

Would they be willing to refer MORE clients to me?

Did I gain credibility from all the testimonials I acquired? Did my giving of myself work?

I think it did. I literally have people banging on my door asking me to write copy for them.

Recap: On the surface, it seems like I gave myself away as a copywriter. Let's reframe that: I SOLD myself as a copywriter. Claude Hopkins said, "The best way to sell anything is to give away a free sample!"

I was selling, through giving!!! Can you think of a MORE POWERFUL method to sell?

I think not.

One of the most powerful engines behind giving is the Law of Reciprocity. It's human nature to want to give back when you receive something for free.

The Hare Krishnas knew that, and had a field day in soliciting funds by walking up to people and putting flowers in their lapel pockets.

Think about it. You'd feel literally OBLIGATED to give back if you were caught in the same situation.

That being said, however, the REAL key to giving is NOT to expect anything in return. You cannot GIVE if you're expecting to get. A gift will cost you something. To qualify as a gift, it MUST cost you something.

The Biblical King David puts this very aptly when he had an issue with burnt offerings and said:

"I will not offer unto the Lord something that costs me nothing!"

It seems paradoxical, but if you give without any expectation, you'll receive MORE because you never did expect anything in return.

Meditate on that.

Lastly, it's not my intention to preach, but something metaphysical happens when you tithe. A tithe is simply offering 10% of your gross income back to society.

In organized religion, it is regarded as giving back 10% to God.

When you do that, you'll not only experience spiritual fulfillment, but it also opens up more gateways for you to receive more abundance into your life. You can see it as good karma.

As an interesting fact, the area of tithing is the only part in the Christian Bible which allows Christians to actually CHALLENGE God by tithing, in Malachi 3:10:

"Bring all the tithes into the storehouse that there may be food in My house, and try Me now in this, says the Lord of hosts, If I will not open for you the windows of heaven and pour out such blessing that there will not be room enough to receive it."

You may or may not subscribe to this, but as my favorite author C.S Lewis puts it so eloquently:

"It's a win/win situation. Either way, you win!"

Selah.

Jo Han Mok is my co-author on the book, "E-Code." He is the Director of my Hypnotic Marketing Institute at http://www.HypnoticMarketingInstitute.com, President of Super Fast Profit Enterprise, and has been featured on America's #1 Personal Development Show alongside Tony Robbins, Mark Victor Hansen and other top achievers, as the

Internet's foremost expert on Joint Venture Marketing. Visit his portal site and find out how Jo Han can help explode your sales and triple your time off in under 7 days. See his main website at http://www.SuperFastProfit.com

The Couple Who Created
A Debt-Free Spiritual Empire

I want to end this book of mine with another story or two, and then a call to action.

The success of Unity Church is another case in point.

Founded in 1889 in Kansas City, Missouri, by Charles and Myrtle Fillmore, Unity School of Christianity is the world headquarters of the Unity movement. After Mrs. Fillmore's remarkable healing using prayer and affirmations, many friends became interested in how she accomplished her healing miracle. From those small prayer circles in living rooms, Unity grew.

Charles and Myrtle Fillmore managed to raise all the money they needed to build and expand their new business. Today Unity Church is a community of people interested in the practical and prosperous messages of the divine. Today their reach expands the globe. They've done it with nothing, and remain debt-free.

It wasn't until 1942 that the real secret of the Fillmore's financial support was revealed. According to Charles Braden's book, *Spirits In*

Rebellion, the Fillmores had created a now-famous "Dedication and Covenant" on December 7, 1892, that reads as follows:

> *We, Charles Fillmore and Myrtle Fillmore, husband and wife, hereby dedicate our selves, our time, our money, all we have and all we expect to have, to the Spirit of Truth, and through it, to the Society of Silent Unity.*
>
> *It being understood and agreed that the said Spirit of Truth shall render unto us an equivalent for this dedication, in peace of mind, health of body, wisdom, understanding, love, life and an abundant supply of all things necessary to meet every want without our making any of these things the object of our existence.*
>
> *In the presence of the Conscious Mind of Christ Jesus, this 7th day of December, 1892 A.D.*

As Charles Braden goes on to explain in his book, "Unity has never put a price upon its services other than a nominal one, because of legal necessity, on its publications…Unity has given freely, and yet there seems always to be money available to meet any obvious need."

What greater proof do you need that trusting in the spiritual laws will provide all you will ever need?

And the greatest of these laws is *giving*.

How To Tell If You Will Be Rich

Do you want to know if you will ever be wealthy?

There's a simple way to find out.

Just answer this question:

***Do you give freely, regularly, generously,
with no expectation of return and with a joyous heart?***

If your answer is *yes*, you are probably *already* wealthy.

If you have a *no* on any part of the question, then take a look at that, release it, and begin to give *freely, regularly, generously, with no expectation of return and with a joyous heart.*

The path is clear.

Giving is the way.

Where Will You Give Today?

Now it's your turn.

Where will you give today?

Ask yourself: *Where did I receive the most joy?*

Write down your answers.

_____

_____

_____

Now, if you want further clarity, or more questions to assist you in knowing where to give money, try these on for size:

Where were you reminded of your divinity?

_____

_____

_____

Where were you encouraged to go for your dreams?

_____

_____

_____

Who made you feel glad to be alive?

_____

_____

_____

Whatever your answers, *that's* where to give your money.

You can give some money to all the people or places you listed above, or you can pick one and give them something now.

And keep these basic principles in mind:

1. Give freely, without expectations.
2. Give anonymously, if at all possible.
3. Give joyously, with a smile.

You are making a difference in the world when you give.

You are making a difference in your own life when you give.

You are making a difference *right now* when you give.

Give!

The 3 Greatest Prosperity
Books Of All Time

I'm fascinated by prosperity.

This past year I read numerous books on the topic. Here are my three favorites:

Seed Money In Action by Jon Speller has stood the test of time. This forty-year-old little booklet has gone through 53 editions, sold 1,000,000 copies, and caused 40,000 people to write the authors and praise it.

The basic message is that as you give, you will receive ten-fold in return. This ancient secret helped create millionaires and billionaires throughout time, and still works today.

There's a catch, of course. You have a give with a mind-set of non-judgmental expectation. When you do, you're in the flow. Most people who are broke are practicing the scarcity principle, not the seed money principle.

Most people who are having money problems would never even think of giving money away, let alone think of the proper way to think

AS they give money away. Yet that's the secret to prosperity in this famous booklet.

Then there's *The Millionaire's Mind* by two authors in a country I never heard of before last year. Two Slovenian authors wrote a book that sold out within 15 days in their country.

When they came to me, I was skeptical. When I read the book, I was amazed. Here's a complete course on how to think like a wealthy person. Long, detailed, practical, and eye-opening, it continues to blow me away.

Do you want to know what happened in the first few hours after I announced the release of that book?

* A German businessman contacted us wanting to start selling this e-book in Germany and building his own website just to promote it to his audience.

* An Indian businessman contacted us wanting to find ways of marketing this e-book in India, and also said: "I got so excited that I decided to mail you right away since I feel this book can help millions here in INDIA."

* A Scandinavian author agent contacted us wanting to translate and publish the book in print and electronic formats in Norway.

*   15 people contacted us immediately wanting to sell this e-book through their websites and e-zines.

*   HUNDREDS of people ordered the book within just five hours of getting the email.

*   Dozens of people wrote from overseas, begging to find a way to pay for the book and get it right NOW.

*   Still others wrote to me, asking if the book would be released in hardcover (not this year).

And all this in just a few hours after I pre-released the e-book.

Is this miraculous or what?

Finally there's the book I co-authored with Stuart Lichtman, called *How to Get Lots of Money For Anything Fast*.

Stuart is a genius. I have never met anyone like him. He has spent at least four decades studying the unconscious mind. The result is that he can pin-point where our unconscious trips us up—and show us how to correct it.

This is incredible. Where before you would set a goal and wonder why you stopped going for it, now you can discover why you stopped yourself—and remove the block. This book really describes how to "get clear," which is a key step in my *Spiritual Marketing* book.

Well, let me throw in one more book on prosperity.

When Tom Pauley wrote his masterpiece, *I'm Rich Beyond My Wildest Dreams, I Am I Am I Am,* he didn't know he would begin a new business.

Since writing that book he has gone on to teach e-classes based on his simple method, give teleseminars, land a publishing contract for the book, and now sell it as an e-book, too. His book is helping people create miracles. His book helped me manifest the home of my dreams.

If you're looking to create prosperity, I suggest you get all of the above titles. They are all e-books so you can have them instantly. They're better reading than the daily newspaper and will lead to far more profit.

Read them and get rich.

<u>Resources</u>:

Seed Money In Action is here:

http://www.mrfire.com/seedmoney.html

The Millionaire Mind is here:

http://hop.clickbank.net/hop.cgi?outrageous/vitale

I'm Rich Beyond My Wildest Dreams is here:

http://hop.clickbank.net/hop.cgi?outrageous/tpauley

How to Get Lots of Money For Anything Fast is here:

http://hop.clickbank.net/hop.cgi?outrageous/fastmoney

About the Author

Joe Vitale is the author of the international #1 best-seller, *Spiritual Marketing*, the #1 best-selling e-book *Hypnotic Writing*, and the #1 best-selling Nightingale-Conant audioprogram, *The Power of Outrageous Marketing*, and numerous other works.

He has also written books for the American Marketing Association and the American Management Association. His most recent book, co-authored with Jo Han Mok, is *The E-Code: 47 Secrets for Making Money Online Almost Instantly*.

Besides being one of the five top marketing specialists in the world today, and the world's first hypnotic writer, Joe is also an ordained minister, a certified metaphysical practitioner, a certified hypnotherapist, and a certified Chi Kung healer. He also holds a doctorate degree in Metaphysical Science.

Dr. Vitale currently lives in the Hill Country outside of Austin, Texas with his pets and his love, Nerissa.

For a catalog of his books and tapes, to read dozens of free articles by him, or to sign up for his popular free e-newsletter, see his main website at http://www.mrfire.com

Printed in the United States
1079400004BB